Contents

Scope and sequence

	Vocabulary 1	Grammar 1	Vocabulary 2	Grammar 2
Welcome to the Rise and Shine Explorers Club	**Numbers 1–20; days of the week; weather:** *cloudy, rainy, sunny, windy*	*This is (Tess). That's (Oscar). It's (Monday / windy).*	**Classroom objects:** *notebook, pen, rubber, ruler*	*This is my (pen). That's my (ruler). How many (pencils)?*
1 Let's explore together	**My things:** *backpack, belt, cap, coat, glasses, scarf, trainers, watch*	*Have you got (a scarf)? Yes, I have. / No, I haven't.*	**Adjectives:** *dark, fair, long, short*	*She's got (long) hair.*
2 Let's be happy at home **Review 1** **Important to me** (Units 1 and 2)	**House:** *bathroom, bedroom, garage, garden, hall, kitchen, living room, stairs*	*Where's (Mum)? She's in (the living room).*	**Furniture:** *bed, lamp, sofa, table*	*Where's (the lamp)? It's on / next to (the table)*
3 Let's explore nature	**Farm animals:** *chicken, cow, donkey, goat, goose, horse, sheep, turkey*	*There's (a goose and a turkey). There isn't (a frog).*	**On the farm:** *bush, fence, rock, wall*	*Where's (the cow)? It's behind (the wall).*
4 Let's try new activities **Review 2** **All about me** (Units 3 and 4)	**Physical activities:** *catch, climb, kick, ride, skate, skip, swim, swing*	*Can you (swim)? Yes, I can. / No, I can't.*	**Activities with *play*:** *play a board game, play football, play tennis, play the guitar*	*Can he play (tennis)? No, he can't. But he can play (the guitar).*
5 Let's share our food	**Food:** *burger, biscuit, carrot, cereal, egg, fish, juice, orange*	*What are you doing? I'm (eating) (an orange).*	**Meal prep:** *cook, grow, make, wash*	*Are you (cooking)? Yes, I am. / No, I'm not.*
6 Let's have holiday fun **Review 3** **Around me** (Units 5 and 6)	**Holiday activities:** *build a sandcastle, collect shells, go on holiday, play on the beach, read comics, sleep*	*I want to (collect shells).*	**Times of day:** *in the morning, in the afternoon, in the evening, at night*	*Do you want to (play) (in the morning)? Yes, I do. / No, I don't.*
Goodbye	*Happy holiday!*			
Celebrations	**Let them shine!:** *balloon, barbecue, cake, candle, present, sparkler* **Beautiful world:** *desert, hill, jungle, mountain, ocean, sky* **Amazing oceans:** *dolphin, octopus, seahorse, seal, shark, whale* **Let them fly!:** *cloud, day, moon, night, star, sun*			

My sounds	Communication	Global Citizen	My Everyday English	Project
th	Describing objects	**I like numbers and maths**	**Giving personal information** *My favourite number is (twenty).*	**My Explorers Club passport**
w, y	Describing people and objects	**I appreciate my community** **Jobs:** *builder, chef, explorer, teacher*	**Commenting on a photo** *Look at this!* *What a nice / great photo!*	**A club book**
l, r	Saying where things are in my house	**I learn about different homes** **Types of homes:** *cave, igloo, tent, treehouse*	**Making suggestions** *Let's put (the pencils) here.* *Good idea!*	**A perfect house plan**
oo, ee	Asking about what there is on a farm	**I learn about the five senses** **Sense verbs:** *hear, see, smell, taste, touch*	**Asking for and giving information** *Excuse me, where's (the café)?* *It's (next to) (the garden).*	**A five senses park map**
i, a	Asking about what people can do	**I know how to enjoy music** **Musical instruments:** *drums, piano, recorder, violin*	**Accepting and declining an invitation** *Would you like to join my club? Yes, of course! / No, thanks.*	**A club poster**
o, i	Talking about what I'm doing now	**I learn about different ingredients** **Food and ingredients:** *butter, flour, fruit, vegetables*	**Going shopping** *I need (carrots).* *OK, let's go shopping!*	**A food truck bar poster**
u, e	Talking about holiday activities	**I stay safe on holiday** **Water safety:** *dangerous, flag, safe, sea*	**Expressing preferences** *I like (the sea).* *I don't. I like (cold weather).*	**A holiday trip plan**
Learning experiences		**Making a 'we are all different' poem** **Making an activity bar chart** **Planning a healthy habits weekend**		

What makes Rise and Shine special?

Lively characters, exciting stories and real-life videos will make your learning experience motivating and fun!

Rise and Shine invites you to discover the world around you, to build cultural awareness, and to help you grow as a responsible global citizen.

Build your passion for learning

Be aware of what you are learning and why through tasks that guide you on your *Time to shine* journey.

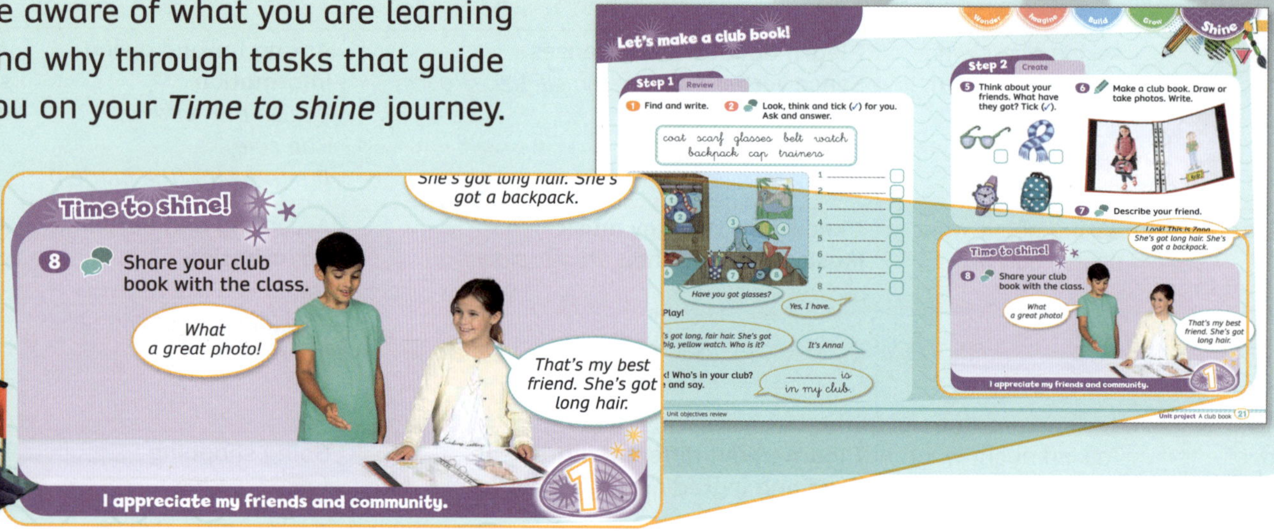

Explore your creativity

Share your curiosity, imagination, creativity and critical thinking through games, activities and puzzles.

Learn at your own pace

With the Pupil's Book, Activity Book, Busy Book and Extra Online Practice you can consolidate your learning at your own pace to achieve exam success.

Grow up as a responsible global citizen

With dedicated Helpers, learn about life, global and local issues through cross-curricular topics, videos, songs and collaborative projects.

Tailor the course to your needs

Rise and Shine is accessible on your computer, tablet and mobile phone. Enjoy your learning experience with the 360º online games and improve your performance each time you play.

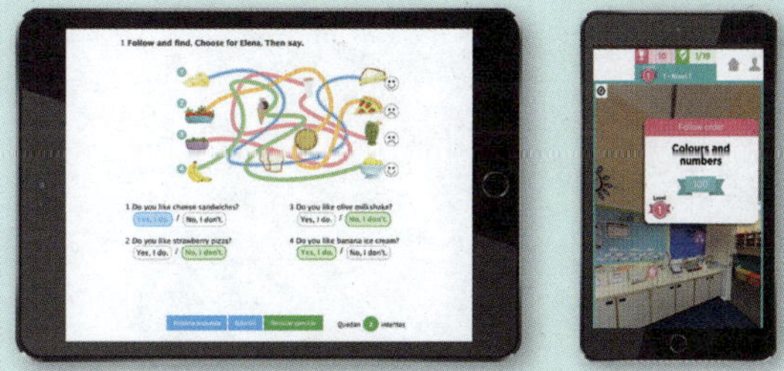

Interactive Pupil's Book & Activity Book with 360º games

Pupil's Book **Activity Book** **Busy Book**

Extra Online Practice

Welcome to the Rise and Shine Explorers Club

Lesson 1

Who do you know?

1 0.04 Listen and explore.

Rise and shine,
It's a beautiful day.
Open your eyes,
Let's learn and play!

Tell me!
What's your friend's name?

2 Point, trace and say.

3 Write your name.

Extra Time Act out and welcome a new member to the Explorers Club.

Lesson 2

1 Sing and act. **Song** (0.05)

1, 2, 3, 4, 5, 6, 7, 8, 9, 10,
11, 12, 13, 14, 15, 16, 17, 18, 19, 20!
Hooray! Hooray! Let's explore today!
Monday, Tuesday, Wednesday, Thursday,
Friday, Saturday, Sunday!
Hooray! Hooray! Let's explore today!

2 Look, think and write. Say.

MONDAY	WEDNESDAY	FRIDAY	SATURDAY
____	____	17	____

I can shine!

3 Choose and say.

Thirteen.

It's Monday.

I can recognise numbers up to 20 and days of the week.

Lesson 3

1 0.07 Listen, point and say.

windy

rainy

sunny

cloudy

2 0.08 Listen or watch.

Let's imagine!

Draw your favourite weather.

I can shine!

3 Look at the story. Number and say.

One. It's cloudy.

 ☐

 ☐

 ☐

 ☐

I can understand a story about the weather.

 Story language *It's (windy).*

Extra Time Play a miming game for your friend to guess the weather.

Lessons 4 and 5

1 0.09 Listen and find.

2 0.10 Listen, read and say.

Chant

What's this?
This is my pen.
What's that?
That's my ruler.

This is my pen.
That's my ruler.

3 0.11 Listen and say. Then write.

My sounds

This and that!
Thank you! Thank you!

I can shine!

4 Play!

I can ask and answer about objects.

Lessons 6 and 7

1 0.13 Listen, write and say.

11	12	13	14	15
eleven	twelve	thirteen	fourteen	fifteen
16	17	18	19	20
sixteen	seventeen	eighteen	nineteen	twenty

2 Count and write.

1 
____

2 
____

3 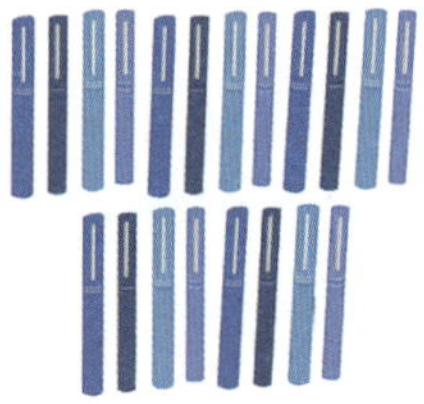
____

4 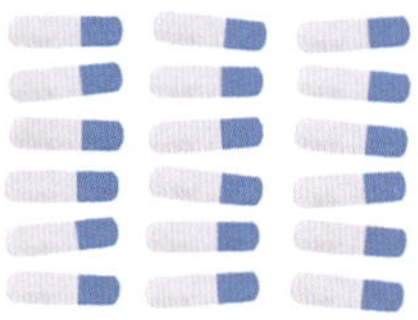
____

Think and share!

Can you count in twos?
10 … 12 … 14 …

I can shine!

3 Play!

How many pencils?

Twelve!

I can ask and answer about how many.

 My Everyday English Asking how many; *How many (pencils)? (Twelve).* **Extra Time** Ask and answer about the objects in your classroom.

My Explorers Club passport

Review

1 Complete.

Favourite day	I like	I've got	Favourite number
Monday			
Tuesday			
Wednesday			
Thursday			
Friday			
Saturday			
Sunday			

My name is ______________.

I'm ______________.

Time to shine!

2 Show and say.

My name is Sam. I'm eight. My favourite day is Saturday. I like tomatoes. I've got a brother. My favourite number is twenty.

Welcome

Let's introduce ourselves!

1 Let's explore together

Lesson 1

Where are the children?

1 (1.01) Listen and explore.

Tell me!
What have you got in your classroom?

2 (1.02) Listen, stick and say.

3 Trace and read. Say.

4 Watch and listen.

I've got a cap.

Extra Time Who has got glasses?

Lesson 2

1 1.03 Sing and act. **Song**

Have you got a backpack and a watch?
Yes, I have. Yes, I have.
Have you got trainers and a coat?
Yes, I have. Yes, I have.
Have you got glasses and a scarf?
Yes, I have. Yes, I have.
Have you got a belt and a cap?
No, I haven't. No, I haven't.

2 1.05 Listen and tick (✓) or cross (✗). Say.

1 
2 
3 

Have you got a scarf?
Yes, I have. / No, I haven't.

I can shine!

3 Ask and answer.

Have you got a watch?

Yes, I have.

I can name my things.

Lesson 3

1 How many? Look at the story. Count and write the number.

belts ☐

backpacks ☐

caps ☐

2 1.07 Listen or watch.

Rise and Shine — Explorers Club

 Story value Working together

Extra Time Draw a picture of a mascot for your class.

I can shine!

3 Circle the club mascot.

a frog

a cat

a butterfly

a rabbit

4 Act out.

I can understand a story about choosing a club mascot.

Let's imagine!

What has the club got?
Is Peanut happy?

Lesson 4

1 1.08 Listen and find.

2 1.09 Listen and number. Say.

3 1.10 Listen, read and say.

She's got long hair.

Chant

She's got long hair.
He's got short hair.
She's got dark hair.
He's got fair hair.

4 Read and match. Then say.

1 

David

2 

Sonia

3 

Veronica

4 

Teo

a She's got long, fair hair.

b He's got short, fair hair.

c He's got short, dark hair.

d She's got long, dark hair.

Extra Time Write a short description of a member of your family.

Lesson 5

1 1.11 Listen and match.

2 Look and play! Add one more.

She's got a short coat and new glasses.

She's got a long belt, too. Blue backpack!

3 1.12 Listen, write and say.

My sounds

It's windy! Look at your yellow watch!

I can shine!

4 Cut out, choose and play!

I can describe my friends and talk about what they've got.

Lesson 6

1 1.15 Listen, look and find. **2** 1.16 Listen, point and say.

3 Circle the odd one out.

1 a  b  c 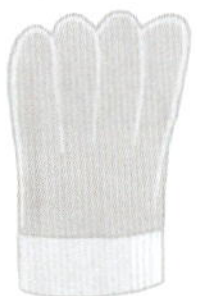

2 a  b  c 

3 a  b 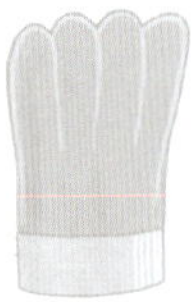 c 

Think and share!
Who's a hero in your community?

4 Watch and listen.

Extra Time Play a miming game for your friend to guess the job.

Lesson 7

Look at my photo!

1 1.17 Listen and write. Then read and number.

1 He's a ______________________.

2 She's a ______________________.

3 He's an ______________________.

4 She's a ______________________.

What a nice photo!

What a great photo!

2 Read. Then write.

Back   Likes 21   Comments 1

posted by Oscar123

This is me and my neighbours.
It's our street party.

Comments

posted by ClaraT

What a ______________________
______________________!

I can shine!

3 Take a photo and say.

Look at this!

Oh, what a great photo!

I can comment on a photo.

Let's make a club book!

Step 1 Review

1 Find and write.

2 Look, think and tick (✓) for you. Ask and answer.

coat scarf glasses belt watch
backpack cap trainers

1 ________ ☐
2 ________ ☐
3 ________ ☐
4 ________ ☐
5 ________ ☐
6 ________ ☐
7 ________ ☐
8 ________ ☐

Have you got glasses?

Yes, I have.

3 Play!

She's got long, fair hair. She's got a big, yellow watch. Who is it?

It's Anna!

4 Think! Who's in your club? Write and say.

________ is in my club.

Step 2 Create

5 Think about your friends. What have they got? Tick (✓).

6 Make a club book. Draw or take photos. Write.

7 Describe your friend.

Look! This is Zana. She's got long hair. She's got a backpack.

Time to shine!

8 Share your club book with the class.

What a great photo!

That's my best friend. She's got long hair.

I appreciate my friends and community.

2 Let's be happy at home

Lesson 1

Where are the children?

1 2.01 Listen and explore.

Tell me!
Where do you live?

2 2.02 Listen, stick and say.

3 Trace and read. Say.

4 Watch and listen.

Extra Time Is Basil's living room big or small?

Lesson 2

1 2.03 **Sing and act.** Song

Where's Peanut?
In the kitchen or the living room?
In the bathroom or the bedroom?
In the garage or on the stairs?
Where's Peanut? He's in the garden!
Yes! Yes! Yes!

2 2.05 **Listen and match. Say.**

1 Mum
2 Dad
3 Granny

a 
b 
c 

Where's Mum?
She's in the living room.

I can shine!

3 **Ask and answer.**

Where's Clara?

She's in the garden.

I can name places in a house.

1 Where's Clara? Look at the story. Tick (✓).

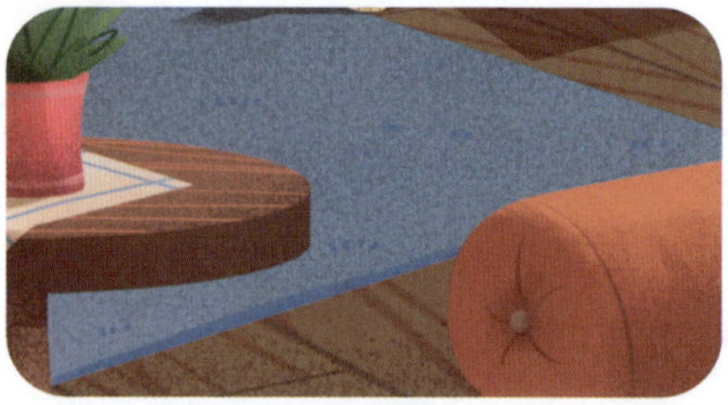

living room ☐

kitchen ☐

garden ☐

2 2.07 Listen or watch.

 Story value Feeling happy at home

Extra Time What does Clara like?

Let's imagine!

What can you do to feel happy at home?

I can shine!

3 Who has a bedroom in the garden? Read and circle.

Basil | Peanut | Clara

4 Act out.

I can understand a story about places in a house.

Lesson 4

1 2.08 Listen and find.

2 2.09 Listen and number. Say.

3 2.10 Listen, read and say.

Chant

Where's the lamp? It's on the table.
Where's the table? It's next to the bed.

Where's the table?
It's next to the bed.

4 Circle four differences. Choose, write and say.

Where's ______________________?
It's ______________________.

Where's ______________________?
It's ______________________.

Lesson 5

1 2.11 Listen and match.

2 Look and play! Add one more.

Where's the lamp?

It's in the bedroom. It's on the table.

3 2.12 Listen, write and say.

My sounds

A red lamp in the living room.

I can shine!

4 Cut out, fold and play!

Where's the cat?

It's in the bedroom. It's on the bed.

I can say where things are in my house.

Lesson 6

1 2.15 Listen, look and find.

2 2.16 Listen, point and say.

3 Which home? Look and write. Say.

1 

2 

3 

4 

1 ____________________

2 ____________________

3 ____________________

4 ____________________

Think and share!

What makes a home?

4 Watch and listen.

Extra Time Look at the pictures. Which places are hot or cold?

Lesson 7

Time to tidy up!

1 2.17 Read. Then listen and write.

To do list

1 tablet on the ____________

2 backpack on the ____________

3 pyjamas on the ____________

2 Choose and write.

pencils books
rulers rubbers
notebooks

To do list

____

____

____

I can shine!

3 Tidy your desk. Say.

I can make suggestions.

Let's design a perfect house plan!

Step 1 Review

bathroom bedroom
living room kitchen stairs
hall garden garage

1 Look and write.

1 
____

2 
____

3 
____

4 
____

5 
____

6 
____

7 
____

8 
____

2 Look and circle. Ask and answer.

Where's the cat? It's in the **garden** / **living room**.

Where's the fish? It's in the **kitchen** / **bedroom**.

3 Play!

Where's the lamp?

It's on the table.

4 What's your favourite room? Write.

I like my ______________________.

Step 2 Create

5 Which homes do you like? Tick (✓) or cross (✗).

6 Make a plan of your perfect house.

7 Decide where to put things in your house.

Let's put the lamp on the table.

Good idea!

Time to shine!

8 Share your house design with the class.

What a great house!

It's a tent house. This is the living room. The sofa is next to the table.

I care about my home.

Review 1 Important to me

1 2.18 Listen and number.

2 Look and point. Then ask and answer.

3 Read and write.

living room   bedroom   garden

1 Where's the ? It's in the ______________.

2 Where's the ? It's in the ______________.

3 Where's the ? It's in the ______________.

Mini-project

4 Complete the checklist for you. Ask and answer.

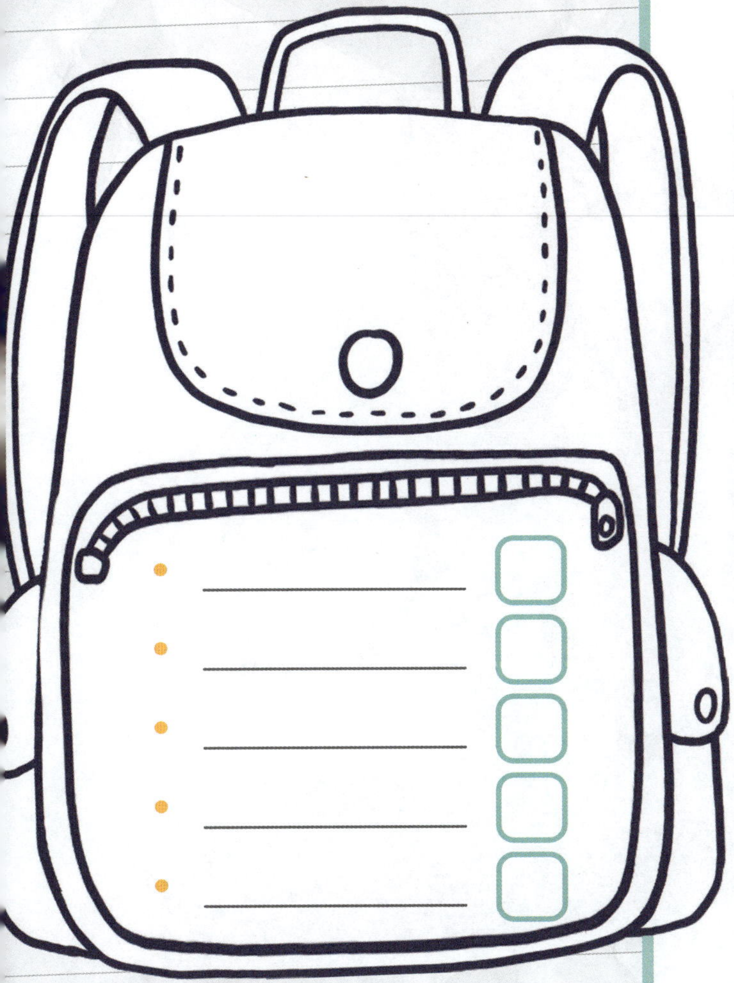

I've got a watch. Have you got a watch?

Yes, I have.

Time to shine!

5 Read and tick (✓).

1 I can read and write words about things and houses. ☐

2 I can talk about my things and my house. ☐

3 I can comment on a photo. ☐

4 I can make suggestions. ☐

6 Vote. Write, say and sing.

My favourite song is	______________
My favourite new word is	______________

3 Let's explore nature

Lesson 1

Where are the children?

1 3.01 Listen and explore.

2 3.02 Listen, stick and say.

3 Trace and read. Say.

4 Watch and listen.

Tell me!
What animals are there where you live?

Extra Time What is Oscar's favourite animal?

Lesson 2

1 3.03 Sing and act. **Song**

There isn't a fox or a duck or a turtle
On the farm, on the farm, on the city farm!
There's a cow and a donkey and a horse, too
On the farm, on the farm, on the city farm!
There's a chicken and a goose and a turkey, too.
On the farm, on the farm!
On the city farm!
There's a sheep and a goat, all for you!
On the farm, on the farm, on the city farm!
On the city farm!

2 3.05 Listen and tick (✓).

a

b

There's a goose and a turkey.
There isn't a frog.

I can shine!

3 Choose, think and say.

It's got four legs. It's white.

A sheep! There's a sheep on the farm.

I can name farm animals.

Lesson 3

1 How many animals? Look at the story. Count and write the number.

four legs ☐ two legs ☐

2 3.07 Listen or watch.

Rise and Shine **Explorers Club**

Extra Time What do you think Peanut eats?

I can shine!

3 Read and match.

horses | chickens | goats

4 Act out.

I can understand a story about farm animals.

Let's imagine!
Where's Peanut?
How do you think he feels?

Lesson 4

1 3.08 Listen and find.

2 3.09 Listen and number. Say.

3 3.10 Listen, read and say.

Where's the cow?
It's behind the wall.

Chant

Where's the cow? It's behind the wall.
Is there a horse behind the wall?
No, there isn't! There's a cow behind the wall!

4 Follow and find. Write and say.

Where's the sheep?

It's behind the rock.

1 There's a ________ behind the ________.

2 There's a ________ behind the ________.

3 There's a ________ behind the ________.

Lesson 5

1 3.11 Listen and number. Say.

a

b

c

2 Look and play! Add one more.

There's a fox on the farm.

Where's the chicken?

It's behind the rock.

Picture c!

3 3.12 Listen, write and say.

My sounds

A goose with boots.
A sheep with teeth!

I can shine!

4 Cut out, choose and play!

Where's the horse?

It's behind the fence.

I can ask and answer about what there is on a farm.

Lesson 6

1 3.15 Listen, look and find.

2 3.16 Listen, point and say.

3 Look and read. Tick (✓) or cross (✗). Then say.

see				
touch				
hear				
taste				
smell				

I can taste an apple!

Think and share!

What's your favourite smell?

4 Watch and listen.

Extra Time In groups, choose a sense to make a poster about it.

Lesson 7

Let's explore the park!

1 3.17 Read and number. Listen and check.

a There's a café next to the garden. ☐

b There's a pond behind the trees. ☐

c There's a playground behind the café. ☐

d There's a city farm next to the playground. ☐

2 Read and write.

1 The ____________ is next to the garden.

2 The ____________ is next to the playground.

3 The ____________ is behind the café.

I can shine!

3 Ask and answer.

I can ask for and give information.

Let's make a five senses park map!

Step 1 Review

1 Find and write.

goat cow horse chicken
goose donkey turkey sheep

1 ______________
2 ______________
3 ______________
4 ______________
5 ______________
6 ______________
7 ______________
8 ______________

2 Look, choose and write. Then say.

There's a ______________ behind the ______________.

3 Point, ask and answer.

Where's the goat?

It's behind the rock.

4 What's your favourite outdoor space near your house? Write.

I like ______________________________.

Step 2 Create

5 What can you do in your park? Tick (✓) or cross (✗).

6 Make a five senses park map. Draw and write.

7 Describe your park.

Look! I can see a turkey. I can smell flowers.

Time to shine!

8 Share your five senses park map with the class.

In my park I can smell flowers. Look! There's a goose next to the bush.

I explore nature. 3

4 Let's try new activities

Lesson 1

Where are the children?

1 (4.01) Listen and explore.

Tell me!
What's your favourite thing to do?

2 (4.02) Listen, stick and say.

3 Trace and read. Say.

4 Watch and listen.

Lesson 2

1 4.03 **Sing and act.** Song

Can you ride a bike? Can you catch a ball?
Can you skate? Can you climb a wall?
Can you swing and swim? Can you kick a ball?
No, I can't! No, I can't.
Try! Try! Try!

Can you ride a bike? No, I can't.
Can you catch a ball? No, I can't.
Can you skate? No, I can't.
Can you climb a wall? No, I can't.
Can you swing and swim? No, I can't.
Can you kick a ball? No, I can't.
Try! Try! Try!
Yes, I can!

2 4.05 **Listen and tick (✓) or cross (✗). Say.**

Can you swim?
Yes, I can. / No, I can't.

I can shine!

3 **Ask and answer.**

Can you skip?

No, I can't.

I can name physical activities.

Lesson 3

1 Who can swim? Look at the story. Tick (✓).

Tess ☐ Oscar ☐ Clara ☐ Basil ☐

2 4.07 Listen or watch.

 Story value Trying new activities

Extra Time Write about what each character can or can't do.

Let's imagine!
What does Oscar want to do?

I can shine!

3 Read. Then write *can* or *can't*.

1 Oscar ________ help Peanut.
2 Tess ________ help Peanut.
3 Clara ________ help Peanut.

4 Act out.

I can understand a story about different activities.

Lesson 4

1 4.08 Listen and find.

2 4.09 Listen and number. Say.

3 4.10 Listen, read and say.

Can he play tennis?
No, he can't.
But he can play the guitar.

Chant

Can she play tennis? Yes, she can!
Can he play football? No, he can't!
But he can play the guitar. Yes, he can!

4 Ask and answer. Complete. Then say.

My friend ______	 ☐	 ☐	 ☐	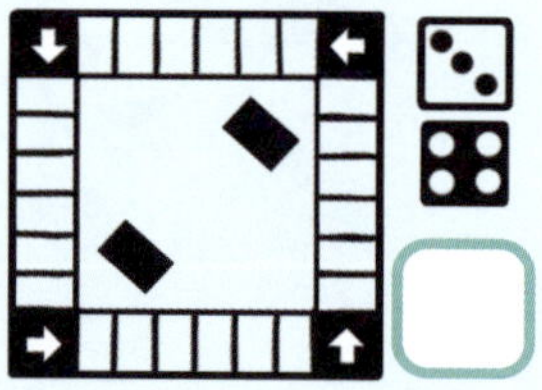 ☐

Can **he** / **she** play football? ______, ______ ______.

Can **he** / **she** play a board game? ______, ______ ______.

Extra Time Play a miming game for your friend to guess the activity.

Lesson 5

1 4.11 Listen and tick (✓) or cross (✗). Say.

2 Look and play! Add one more.

Can he play tennis?

No, he can't. But he can skate!

3 4.12 Listen, write and say.

My sounds

She can't ride a bike, but she can play a game!

I can shine!

4 Cut out, write and play!

I can ask and answer about what others can do.

Lesson 6

1 4.15 Listen, look and find.

2 4.16 Listen and number.

3 Read and tick (✓).

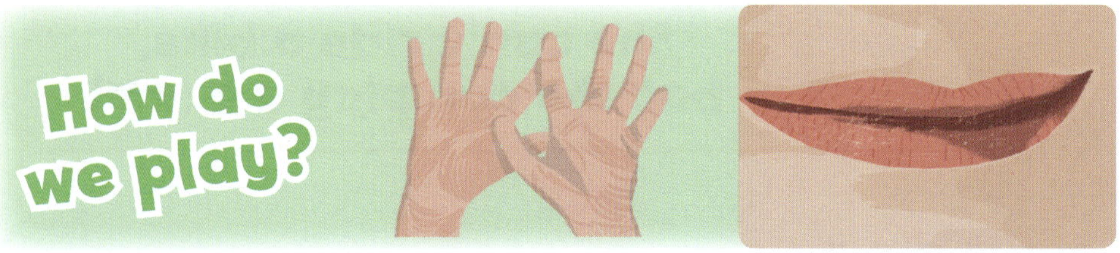

piano		
drums		
recorder		
violin		
guitar		

Think and share!
What's your favourite musical instrument?
Can you play it?

4 Watch and listen.

Extra Time Think of other musical instruments. How can you play them?

Lesson 7

Invitations

1 Read. Then listen and complete. (4.17)

After-school club

Join my club on __________ after school!
At the club, you can
- play the guitar ☐
- play tennis ☐
- play board games ☐

Would you like to join my club? Yes / No

2 Who's joining the club? Read and tick (✓).

☐ *Hi, I'm Ben! I'd like to join a tennis club.*

☐ *Hi, I'm Jack! I'd like to join a music club.*

☐ *Hi, I'm Teo! I'd like to join a football club.*

3 Read and complete.

Join my club!

Name: ____________________

I can come on:
Mon / Tues / Wed
Thurs / Fri

I'd like to play:
tennis / football / drums
the recorder / board games

I can shine!

4 Ask and answer.

I can accept and decline an invitation.

Let's plan a club poster!

Step 1 Review

1 Find and write.

2 Look, think and tick (✓) for you.

ride skip swing climb
skate kick catch swim

1 ______ ☐

2 ______ ☐

3 ______ ☐

4 ______ ☐

5 ______ ☐

6 ______ ☐

7 ______ ☐

8 ______ ☐

3 Point, ask and answer.

Can he play the guitar?

No, he can't. But he can play board games.

4 What can you do best? Write.

I can ______________________ .

Step 2 Create

5 Plan your club. Tick (✓).

6 Create a poster for your club. Draw and write.

7 Invite friends to join your club.

Would you like to join my club?

Time to shine!

8 Share your club poster with the class.

I can try new activities.

Review 2 All about me

1 4.18 **Listen and number.**

Where?

It's behind the wall.

2 **Look and point. Then say.**

3 **Read, match and write.**

1 Can you skate?

____

2 Can you climb the wall?

____

3 Can you ride a bike?

____

Yes, I can.
No, I can't.

a

b

c

Mini-project

4 Draw and write.

a

There's a ________.

There isn't a ________.

5 Listen to your friend and draw.

b

Time to shine!

6 Read and tick (✓).

1 I can read and write farm animals and action words. ☐

2 I can talk about farm animals and physical activities. ☐

3 I can ask for and give information. ☐

4 I can accept and decline an invitation. ☐

7 Vote. Write, say and sing.

My favourite song is	________
My favourite new word is	________

5 Let's share our food

Lesson 1

Where are the children?

1 5.01 Listen and explore.

Tell me!
What's your favourite vegetable?

2 5.02 Listen, stick and say.

3 Trace and read. Say.

He's got a carrot.

4 Watch and listen.

Extra Time What food has Stella got?

Lesson 2

1 5.03 Sing and act. Song

What are you doing? I'm eating!
Burgers, carrots, fish and eggs!
What are you doing? I'm eating!
Cereal, biscuits and oranges, too!
What are you doing?
I'm drinking orange juice!
I'm drinking orange juice, and so are you!

2 5.05 Listen and tick (✓). Then say.

What are you doing?
I'm eating an orange.

I can shine!

3 Mime, ask and answer.

What are you doing?

I'm eating a burger.

I can name food.

Lesson 3

1 What is Oscar eating? Look at the story. Tick (✓).

soup ☐	a salad ☐	a sandwich ☐	a biscuit ☐

2 5.07 Listen or watch.

Rise and Shine **Explorers Club**

 Story value Sharing food

Extra Time Draw a salad dish for Peanut and label it.

Let's imagine!

How are the children helping Stella? How do you think they feel?

I can shine!

3 What's in Clara's soup? Tick (✓).

- a pizza and eggs ☐
- tomatoes and salad ☐
- carrots and tomatoes ☐

4 Act out.

I can understand a story about preparing food.

Lesson 4

1 5.08 **Listen and find.**

2 5.09 **Listen and number. Say.**

3 5.10 **Listen, read and say.**

Are you cooking?
Yes, I am. / No, I'm not.

Chant

Are you cooking? Are you eating? Yes, I am. Yes, I am!
Are you washing? Are you drinking? No, I'm not. No, I'm not!

4 **Follow, read and write. Ask and answer.**

1 Are you ______________ an egg?

2 Are you ______________ tomatoes?

3 Are you ______________ a carrot?

4 Are you ______________ a sandwich?

Extra Time Make a list of collocations with the verbs and foods.

Lesson 5

1 5.11 Listen and tick (✓). Say.

2 Choose, mime and play! Add one more.

What are you doing?

I'm washing tomatoes.

Are you making a salad?

Yes, I am!

3 5.12 Listen, write and say.

My sounds

An orange in a pot.
A fish on a dish!

I can shine!

4 Cut out, make and play!

Are you cooking?

No, I'm not. I'm washing the carrots. I'm making a salad.

I can talk about what I'm doing now.

Lesson 6

1 5.15 Listen, look and find.

2 5.16 Listen and number. Say.

3 Read and circle. Say. Can you add more?

I want...	I need...
pizza	flour butter fruit vegetables ______
sandwich	flour butter fruit vegetables ______
juice	flour butter fruit vegetables ______
soup	flour butter fruit vegetables ______

Think and share!
What food is good for you?

4 Watch and listen.

Extra Time Think of a dish you want to cook and make the shopping list.

Shopping

Lesson 7

1 5.17 Read, listen and tick (✓) or cross (✗).

tomatoes ☐
apple juice ☐
eggs ☐
cereal ☐

2 And you? Circle and write.

Shopping list

oranges / apples / strawberry juice

carrots / tomato soup

____

____

I can shine!

3 Let's go shopping!

I can shop for food.

Let's create a food truck bar poster!

Step 1 Review

1 Find and write.

2 What food do you like? Tick (✓).

fish burgers carrots oranges
juice cereal biscuits eggs

1 ______
2 ______
3 ______
4 ______
5 ______
6 ______
7 ______
8 ______

3 Read and write. Ask and answer.

1 I'm growing ______.
2 I'm making ______.
3 I'm washing ______.
4 I'm cooking ______.

What are you doing?

4 Think! Choose and write food for your food truck bar.

______ ______ ______

Step 2 Create

5 Write a shopping list.

6 Create your food truck bar poster.

7 Tell your friend what you need.

I need vegetables: tomatoes, carrots and olives!

Time to shine!

8 Share your food truck bar poster with the class.

I can share food with friends. 5

6 Let's have holiday fun

Lesson 1

What are they doing?

1 6.01 Listen and explore.

Tell me!
What things can you collect?

2 6.02 Listen, stick and say.

3 Trace and read. Say.

4 Watch and listen.

Extra Time What is Clara eating?

Lesson 2

1 6.03 Sing and act. Song

I want to play on the beach with my friends.
I want to build a sandcastle!
I want to play on the beach with my friends.

I want to collect shells and rocks.
I want to swim and climb!
I want to collect shells and rocks.

I want to read comics and sleep.
I want to have a good time!
I want to read comics and sleep.
I want to go on holiday!

2 6.05 Listen and number. Say.

a b c d

I want to collect shells.

I can shine!

3 Choose and say.

I want to build a sandcastle.

Me too!

I can name holiday activities.

6 build a sandcastle

Lesson 3

1 What is Tess doing? Look at the story. Tick (✓).

1 She's reading comics. ☐
2 She's building a sandcastle. ☐
3 She's collecting shells. ☐

2 6.07 Listen or watch.

 Story value Having fun with friends

Extra Time Think of other activities you can do at the beach and draw a picture.

I can shine!

Let's imagine!
Who turns the Explorers Club into a beach? Why?

3 Who says what? Write and say.

collect build play

1 I want to ________ football.
2 I want to ________ shells.
3 I want to ________ a sandcastle.

4 Act out.

I can understand a story about holiday activities.

Lesson 4

1 6.08 Listen and find. **2** 6.09 Listen and tick (✓). Say.

3 6.10 Listen, read and say.

Do you want to play in the morning? Yes, I do. / No, I don't.

Chant

Do you want to play in the morning? Yes, I do!
Do you want to play in the afternoon? Yes, I do!
Do you want to play in the evening? Yes, I do!
Do you want to play at night? No, I don't! I want to sleep!

4 Follow and write. Ask and answer.

1 Do you want to ________________ in the morning?
2 Do you want to ____________ in the ____________ ?
3 Do you want to ________________ in ____ evening?

Lesson 5

1 6.11 Listen and match. Then tick (✓) for you and say.

1 

2 

3 

morning

afternoon

evening

4 

5 

6 

2 Choose, mime and play!

Do you want to collect shells in the morning?

Yes, I do.

3 6.12 Listen, write and say.

My sounds

The sun is out, let's have fun.
It's cold and wet, let's go to bed!

I can shine!

4 Cut out, ask and answer.

I can talk about what I want to do on holiday.

Lesson 6

1 6.15 Listen, look and find.

2 6.16 Listen and number.

sea | flag | safe | dangerous

3 Look and write *S* (safe) or *D* (dangerous). Say.

1 

2 

3 

4 

Think and share!
Do you prefer cold or hot weather on holiday?

4 Watch and listen.

Extra Time How do you protect yourself from the sun?

Lesson 7

Going on holiday

1 6.17 Listen and read. Then circle.

Dear Grandad,

This holiday is great!
I'm playing on the beach, building sandcastles and swimming in the sea.
The weather is hot and sunny.

Miss you,

Jake

1

2

3

2 Read and complete.

Dear ________,

I **like** / **don't like** my holiday! The weather is ________ and ________.

I'm ________ and ________.

See you soon,

____

I can shine!

3 Let's go on holiday!

I can talk about my preferences.

Let's plan a holiday trip!

Step 1 Review

1 Find and write. 2 What activities do you like? Tick (✓).

comics holiday build shells
collect sandcastles beach sleep

1 go on ________________ ☐
2 read ________________ ☐
3 ________________ ☐
4 play on the ________ ☐
5 ________ ________ ☐
6 ________ ________ ☐

3 Read and write. Ask and answer.

1 In the morning, I want to
________________________________.

2 In the afternoon, I want to
________________________________.

Do you want to sleep in the morning on holiday?

4 Choose and say.

I like ________ weather on holiday.

Step 2 Create

5 Think of activities. Write.

Monday

Morning ______________

Afternoon ______________

Tuesday

Morning ______________

Afternoon ______________

6 Create your holiday trip plan. Draw and write.

7 Describe your holiday trip plan.

I want to sleep in the afternoon!

Time to shine!

8 Share your holiday trip plan with the class.

I can plan holiday fun with friends. 6

Review 3 Around me

1 6.18 Listen and number.

2 Look and point. Then ask and answer.

3 Read, write and match.

collect build read

a

b

c

1 I want to ____________ a sandcastle. ☐

2 I want to ____________ shells. ☐

3 I want to ____________ a comic. ☐

Mini-project

4 Create a sign for the Explorers Club.

Time to shine!

5 Read and tick (✓).

1 I can read and write food and holiday words.

2 I can talk about food and holiday activities.

3 I can talk about what I'm doing now.

4 I can talk about my preferences.

6 Vote. Write, say and sing.

My favourite song is	____________
My favourite new word is	____________

Goodbye from the Rise and Shine Explorers Club

What is Oscar doing?

1 7.01 Listen and explore.

2 7.02 Listen again and tick (✓).

3 Watch.

Extra Time What has Peanut got?

4 7.03 **Sing and act.** Song

Goodbye, Stella, Tess and Clara,
Basil, Oscar and Peanut, too!
It's holiday time and I'm an explorer!
Lots of things to see and do!
Goodbye! Goodbye!
Happy holiday to you!

I can shine!

5 **Draw you as an explorer. Then say.**

I'm an explorer! I want to collect shells.

What a great picture!

Level 2

Let them shine!

What can you see?

1 8.01 Listen and number. Say.

2 8.02 Sing and act. Listen again and circle. Song

It's your birthday, let's have fun!
A cake and a sparkler for everyone!
Happy birthday, happy birthday, happy birthday to you!
A watch, a backpack, a book and a ball!
Thank you for my presents! I like them all!
Happy birthday, happy birthday, happy birthday to you!

3 Make a sparkler decoration. Say.

Have you got a sparkler?

Yes, I have. Look!

Beautiful world

What can you see?

1 8.05 Listen and number. Say.

2 8.06 Sing and act. Listen again and circle. Song

This is a beautiful world! How can it be?
Turtles in the ocean and fish in the sea!
Animals on mountains and hills and in trees!
This is a beautiful world! Do you know why?
Animals in the jungle, in the desert, in the sky!

3 Make a beautiful world. Say.

I love the ocean!

I like mountains!

Amazing oceans

What can you see?

1 8.09 Listen and number. Say.

2 8.10 Sing and act. Song

What can you see in the ocean?
At the bottom of the deep blue sea?
Can you see a seahorse?
Yes! Yes! Yes!
I can see a seahorse, an octopus,
a dolphin and a seal!
A shark and a whale – at the
bottom of the deep blue sea!

Ocean animals which start with the letter *s*:

____

____

____

3 Make an ocean scene. Say.

What's in your ocean?

There's an octopus!

Let them fly!

What can you see?

1 8.13 Listen and number. Say.

2 8.14 Sing and act. Listen again and write *D* (day) or *N* (night).

Song

I'm flying a kite.
I can see the sun!
I can see clouds in the sky!
It's day and I'm flying a kite.
Fly, kite, fly!
I'm flying a kite.
I can see the moon.
I can see stars in the sky.
It's night and I'm flying a kite.
Fly, kite, fly!

sun ☐ clouds ☐
moon ☐ stars ☐

3 Make a kite. Say.

I like your kite!

Thank you!

Learning experience 1

Making a 'we are all different' poem

Step 1 Start!

Remember!

1 Write *a*, *e*, *i* or *o*. Point and say.

I've got a coat.

I'm in the kitchen.

1  c o a t

2  g _ rd _ n

3  k _ tch _ n

4  l _ ng, d _ rk h _ _ r

5  sc _ rf

6  l _ v _ ng r _ _ m

Step 2 Think!

2 Look and match. Ask and answer.

Have you got a cap?

Yes, I have.

You are Scarlett.

Appreciate diversity.

cap

bedroom

dark hair

fair hair

1 

2 

garden

short hair

long hair

glasses

Home-school link

Find some photos. Talk to your family about what the people have.

Sustainable Development Goals
10
Reduced inequalities

Context: personal / social

Future skill: friendship

Sustainable Development Goal: understand we're all different

Step 3 Create!

3 Look, read and write the names.

a

Hello! I'm ____________ .
I've got short, dark hair.
I've got glasses.
I'm in the bedroom.

Different! Yes, we are!
That's cool! Yeah!

b

Hello! I'm ____________ .
I've got long, fair hair.
I've got a cap.
I'm in the garden.

Different and friends!
That's cool! Yeah!

4 Write your own poem.

Digital Resources
Resource a puzzle poem
PDF

5 In pairs, read your poem out loud to the class.

This is our poem 'We are all different'.

Step 4 Peer review!

6 Think and say.

What a nice poem!
Being different is cool!
Let's make a new poem together!

Reflection Time

- [ ] I can use my things and house words.
- [ ] I can describe a photo.
- [ ] I can have new friends.

Learning experience 2

Making an activity bar chart

Step 1 Start!

Remember!

1 Find the words. Point and say.

playthedrumsrecorderrockrideahorseskatewallboardgame

1 
2 
3 
4 
5 
6 
7 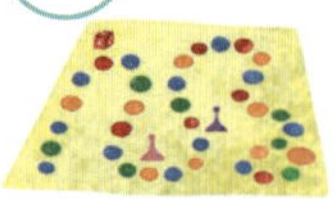

I can play the drums.

There's a recorder.

Step 2 Think!

Learn from each other.

2 Ask and answer. Count and write.

Can Shui ride a horse?

Yes, she can.

	Shui	Boris	Hazel	Karim	TOTAL
1 Can you ride a horse?	✓	✗	✗	✗	1
2 Can you swim?	✗	✓	✓	✓	
3 Can you kick a ball?	✓	✓	✓	✓	
4 Can you climb a wall?	✓	✗	✓	✗	

Home-school link

Talk to your family about what you can learn from each other.

Sustainable Development Goals 4
Quality education

Context: personal / social

Future skill: team spirit

Sustainable Development Goal: have the opportunity to learn things

Step 3 *Create!*

3 Look, read and colour.

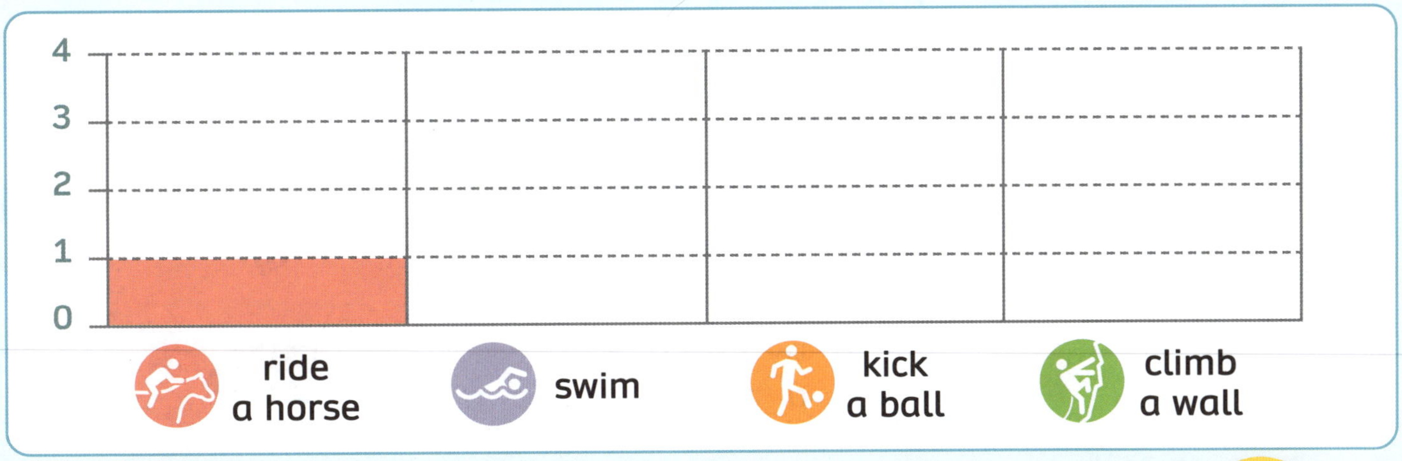

4 Make your own activity questionnaire and bar chart.

Resources
a questionnaire
a bar chart
Digital Resources
PDF

5 Present your activity bar chart to the class.

I'm Shui. I can ride a horse. But Boris, Hazel and Karim can't.

Step 4 *Peer review!*

6 Think and say.

You can do nice activities.
You can't climb, but I can teach you.
I can't skip, but you can teach me.
We can learn together!

Reflection Time

- [ ] I can use action words.
- [ ] I can show information in a chart.
- [ ] I can teach and learn new things.

Learning experience 3

Planning a healthy habits weekend

Step 1 Start!

Remember!

1 Find the words. Point, ask and answer.

What do you want to eat?

1 

2 

3 

4 

b	o	a	r	d	g	a	m	e	a
i	r	s	d	f	g	e	i	v	t
s	a	g	c	a	r	m	z	u	s
c	n	k	v	c	e	r	e	a	l
u	g	u	b	o	j	l	d	a	s
i	e	q	e	m	e	f	p	h	l
t	p	n	l	i	c	i	o	n	e
s	a	n	d	c	a	s	t	l	e
h	o	a	n	l	w	h	l	o	p

What do you want to do?

5 

6 

7 

8 

Step 2 Think!

Care for oneself.

2 What is Emma doing on Saturday? Look and read.

In the morning, I want to have orange juice and...

Emma's healthy habits weekend!

	SATURDAY
In the morning	I want to have  and an  with  for breakfast.
In the afternoon	I want to build a  with my friend Jack.
In the evening	I want to play  with my family.

Home-school link

Talk to your family about your favourite weekend activities.

Sustainable Development Goals 3
Good health and well-being

Context: personal

Future skill: planning things

Sustainable Development Goal: have a healthy lifestyle

Step 3 Create!

3 Read and circle.

1 Hello, I'm Emma. Today it's Sunday. I want to have milk and cereal for breakfast.

a  b 

2 In the afternoon, I want to play football with my school team.

a  b 

3 In the evening, I want to play the guitar with my sister.

a  b 

4 Plan your own healthy habits weekend.

Digital Resources
Resource a timetable
PDF

5 Present your healthy habits weekend timetable to the class.

Hello! I'm Emma. This is my healthy habits weekend timetable.

Step 4 Peer review!

6 Think and say.

You are very healthy!
Your activities are real fun!
You care for yourself. Well done!

Reflection Time

- [ ] I can use food, times of the day and action words.
- [ ] I can understand a timetable.
- [ ] I can care for myself.

Grammar

Welcome to the Rise and Shine Explorers Club	**Grammar 1** **This is** (Tess). **That's** (Oscar). **It's** (Monday / windy).	**Grammar 2** **This is my** (pen). **That's my** (ruler). **How many** (pencils)?
1 Let's explore together	**Grammar 1** **Have you got** (a scarf)? Yes, **I have**. / No, **I haven't**.	**Grammar 2** **She's got** (long) hair.
2 Let's be happy at home	**Grammar 1** **Where's** (Mum)? **She's in** (the living room).	**Grammar 2** **Where's** (the lamp)? **It's on / next to** (the table).
3 Let's explore nature	**Grammar 1** **There's** (a goose and a turkey). **There isn't** (a frog).	**Grammar 2** **Where's** (the cow)? **It's behind** (the wall).
4 Let's try new activities	**Grammar 1** **Can you** (swim)? Yes, **I can**. / No, **I can't**.	**Grammar 2** **Can he** play (tennis)? No, **he can't. But he can** play (the guitar).
5 Let's share our food	**Grammar 1** **What are you doing?** **I'm (eating)** (an orange).	**Grammar 2** **Are you (cooking)?** Yes, **I am**. / No, **I'm not**.
6 Let's have holiday fun	**Grammar 1** **I want to** (collect shells).	**Grammar 2** **Do you want to** (play) (in the morning)? Yes, **I do**. / No, **I don't**.

My progress chart

	Welcome	Unit 1	Unit 2	Unit 3	Unit 4	Unit 5	Unit 6
Listening	I can recognise my words.	I can hear my words in dialogues.		I can listen to descriptions and information.		I can understand my phrases and sentences in dialogues.	
Reading	I can recognise my words.	I can recognise my phrases and sentences in short stories.		I can read short stories and descriptions.		I can read short stories and notice detailed information.	
Speaking	I can say my words and phrases.	I can describe people and things.		I can ask and answer questions about the world around me.		I can talk about myself and my world.	
Writing	I can make marks and write numbers.	I can trace and copy my words.		I can write my words and phrases.		I can write my sentences.	

Rise and Shine cut-outs

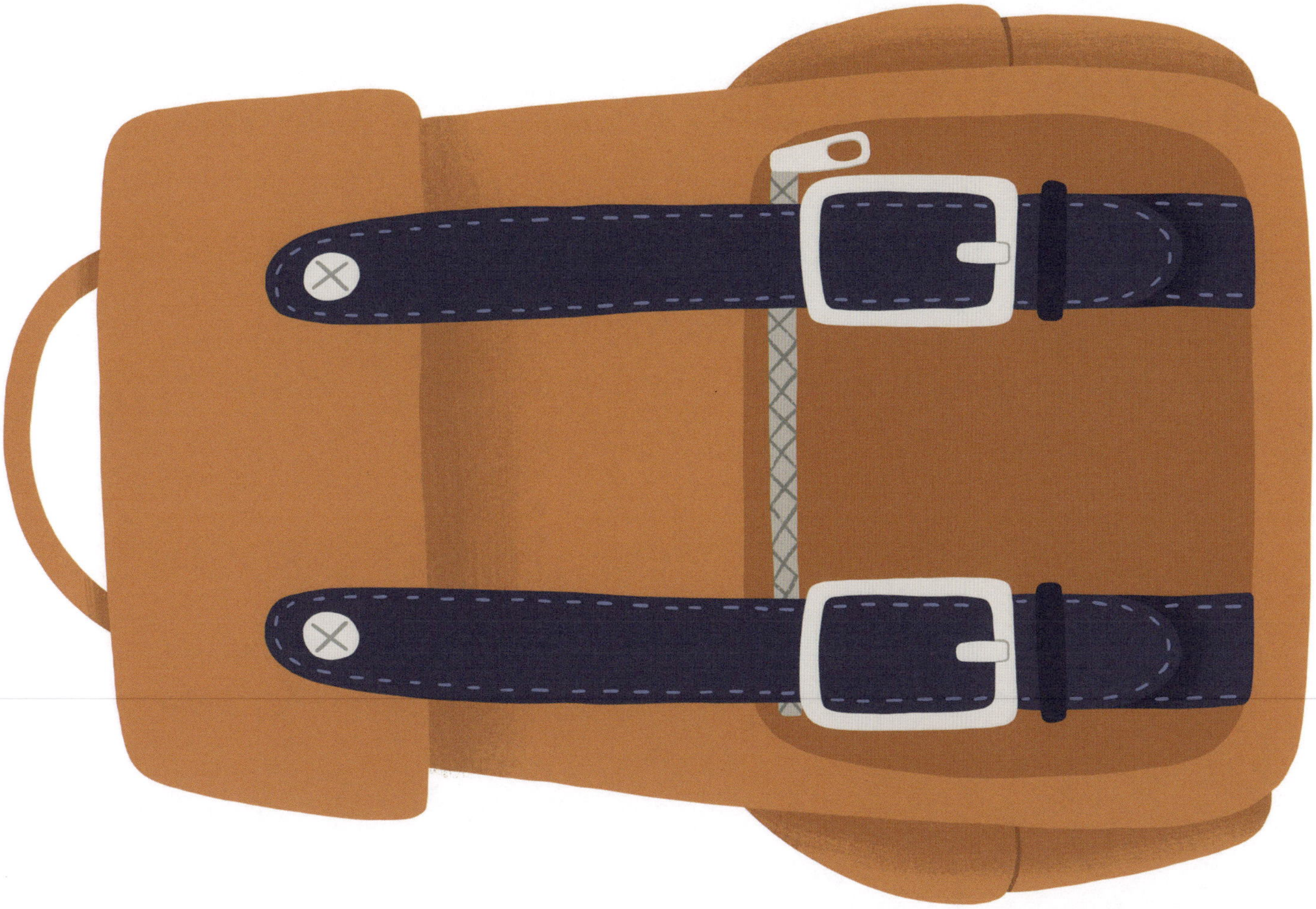

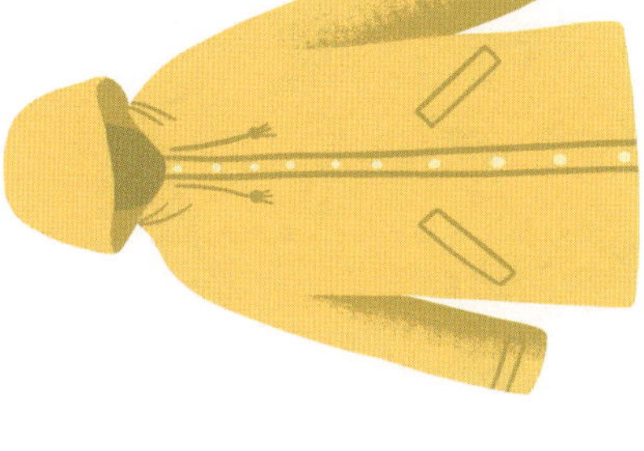

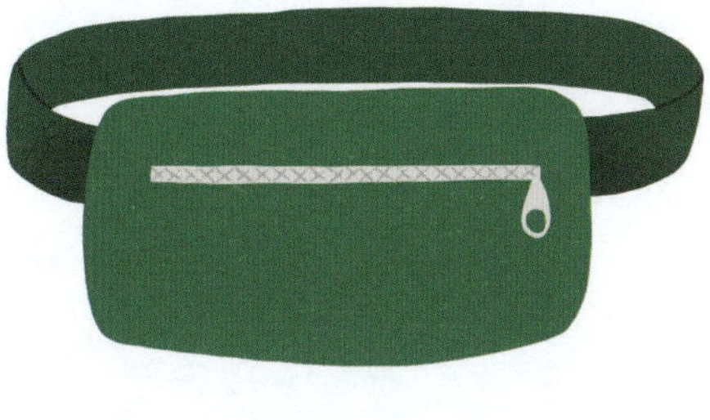

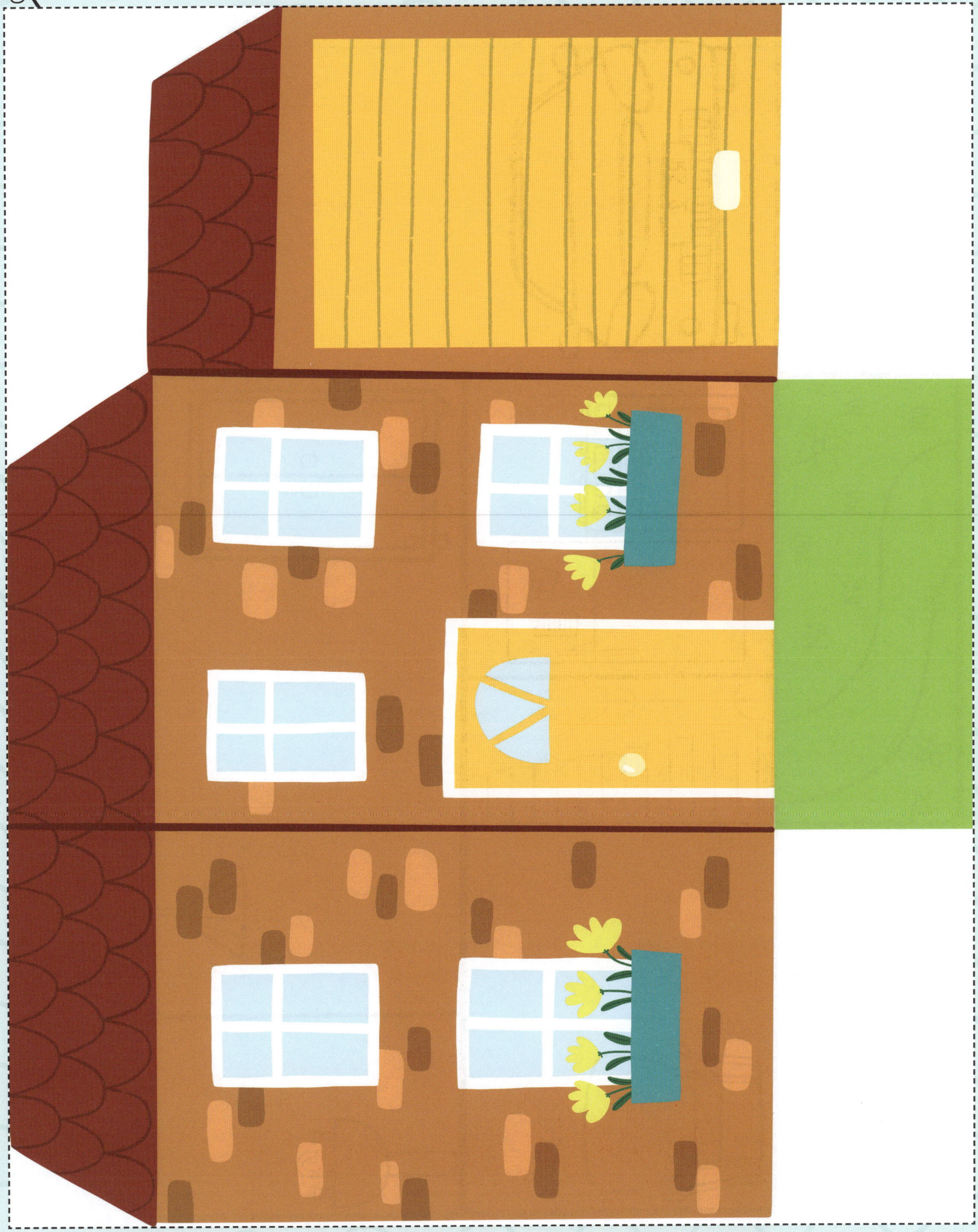

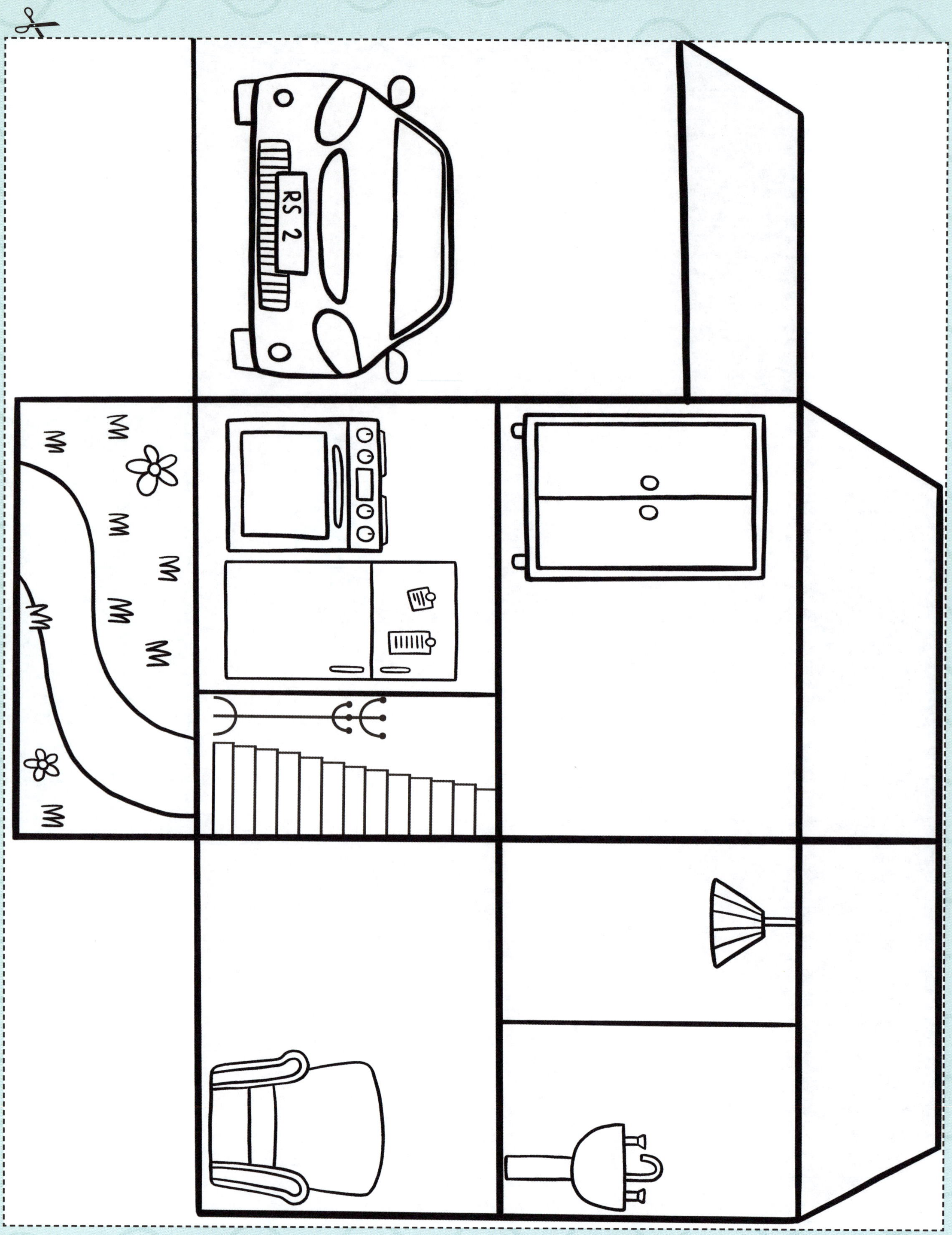
RS 2

——— fold ---------- cut

Name:
swim
play the guitar
CLIMB
skate
PLAY FOOTBALL

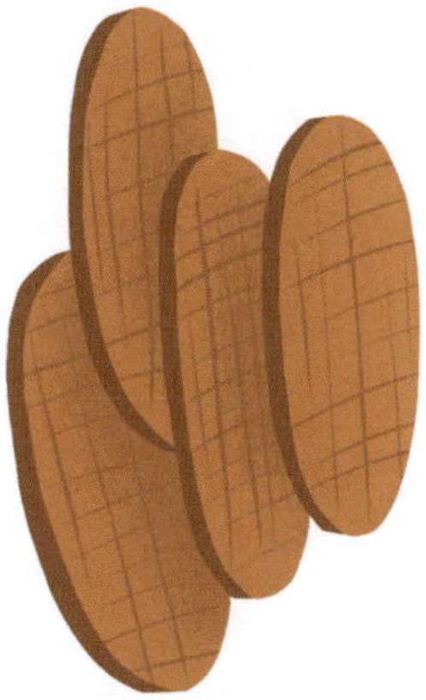

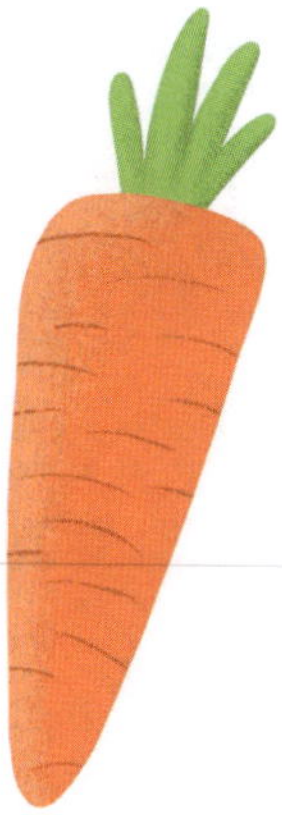
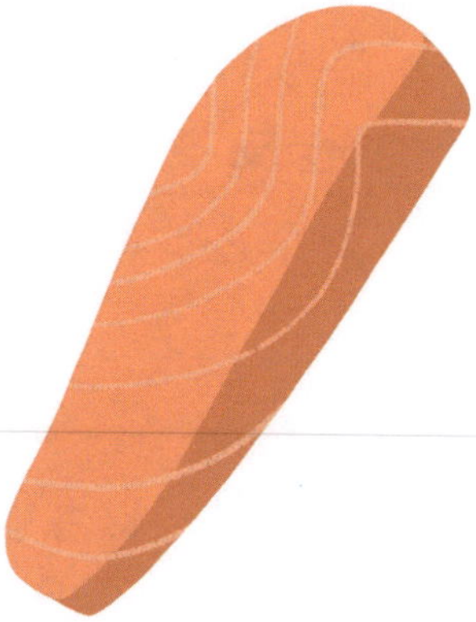
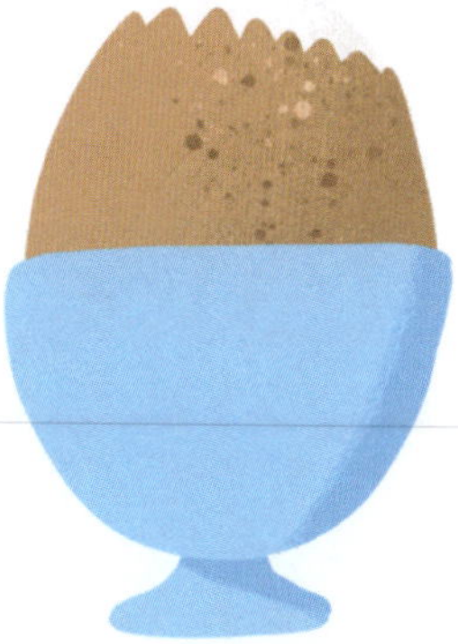

SUPER
BOY
KIDS FUN

Rise and Shine stickers

Unit 1

pages 12–13

Unit 2

pages 22–23

Unit 3

pages 34–35

Unit 4

pages 44–45

Unit 5

pages 56–57

Unit 6

pages 66–67